AMANDA M RENAUD

AUTHOR AND LEADERSHIP ADVISOR

Exceptional Minds

Legal Disclaimer

DEDICATION

I would like to dedicate this book to my deceased sister Alexandra

Renaud 1990-2013, who's life ended suddenly. My younger sister was

my best friend and a true leader and wonderful mother. Alexandra will

be missed and is loved by so many.

ACKNOWLEDGEMENTS

I would like to thank my mother, Leighanna, for all her wonderful support and encouragement. Thank you, mom, for demonstrating leadership through adversity to all of us girls our entire lives and always believing in us.

I would like to acknowledge my Mentor and Publisher, Robert J Moore, who has given me the opportunity to succeed and pursue my dreams.

Lastly, I want to acknowledge my family and Robert's publishing team for their continued support and hard work. Thank you so much for all your efforts.

TABLE OF CONTENTS

Contents

FOREWORD

Amanda M Renaud has created an epic book in *Exceptional Minds*. She has captured all the key elements for success, showing how essential the correct mindset is when in a position of leadership.

Not only does she explain the importance of critical thinking, but gives examples from her own experience on the value of character traits such as resilience, integrity, compassion, and empathy, when combined with goal setting, and support for staff which make for a solid foundation for change and accomplishment.

Amanda stresses the fact that those with exceptional minds are always observant to understand the needs of each employee in order to provide training and encouragement so that they experience growth and empowerment resulting in their actions being in alignment with the company's objectives and goals.

Amanda also addresses toxicity in the workplace which leads to high turnover and how to deal with it. She points out that surrounding yourself with highly motivated people who practise self-care and balance allows you to be innovative and success-oriented.

In addition to negative toxicity, Amanda introduces us to the detrimental effects of positive toxicity which include minimizing other's feelings leaving them feeling unheard and invalidated. This creates barriers and breakdowns in communication, transparency and trust, which Amanda shows how to correct.

Furthermore, Amanda tackles the hard issues of ego and power struggles, control, and emotional issues as well as the "Thieves of Success" and what can be done to combat and defeat them.

These are only a few of the excellent discussions that *Exceptional Minds* provides for empowering us as entrepreneurs and business leaders.

Again, let me congratulate Amanda on this excellent, well-written and highly enlightening business resource.

Robert J Moore

Director, Just Like Family Home Care

Serving Belleville, Kingston, Peterborough and Surrounding Areas

(613) 902-7374

mideasternontario@justlikefamily.ca

Introduction

We are individuals in a fast-paced and growing society that keeps evolving daily. There is a need for more influential and powerful statuses in society, which are highly desired by many people all over the globe. The biggest push we strive for in our everyday roles is the exceptional mindset that leads us to success and comfort.

Often, we wonder how to navigate through life feeling more satisfied and have better quality interactions with life around us. Exceptional Minds often have unique life experiences and many attributes and commonalities. Many have never really taken the time to see what an exceptional mindset looks like and how we achieve this in order to achieve all our goals and deepest desires.

When we identify who we are, bring awareness to ourselves and commit to growth, success is just around the corner. If you find yourself trying to maintain and balance life well, meeting societal standards, you may need to identify, appreciate, and acknowledge that perhaps you have or could have the framework and concepts of the exceptional mindset.

The most important factors to our success are our own personal standards, morals, goals and skill sets. Exceptional-minded beings are forever seeking opportunities, growth, and knowledge, and within this literature, you will begin to understand yourself a bit more while growing and creating an awareness that can benefit ourselves, workplaces, relationships and the overall journey of life.

Amanda M Renaud

Chapter 1

A GLIMPSE OF THE EXCEPTIONAL MIND

Exceptional Minded individuals seek to enhance their social status and roles. These individuals often spend long hours participating in virtual rallies and conferences. They are always planning and educating themselves as well as continuing to learn and grow. They seek to hear diverse opinions in the business world.

They take skills from leaders and individualize what works for them as a representation of that mindset. Most exceptional-minded individuals are busy-minded in general. We find ourselves cluttering our brains which are often filled with tasks, goals and new ways to be innovative and define ourselves through our interests and passions. These individuals tend to be in care giver roles and leadership roles from all walks of life. Our minds are filled with endless ideas and creativity.

We often find ourselves frustrated with others for not diving into our new-found glories and adventures. I feel like a lot of people question whether they're overwhelmed, uninspired or just flat-out exhausted with thinking and doing. We are usually individuals of many skills and interests, as we often project diversity in our interests and desires. All of this sounds great, and it can offer steps toward a more balanced future.

An exceptional mind is often prone to exhaustion and tedious task-orientated goals, but the compassion and drive they possess are what makes them exceptional. The issue with task-orientated goals is they often don't change our character and aren't as fulfilling. Fulfillment of task-orientated goals is often redundant and short-term.

An example of this type of task-orientated goal is building a new piece of furniture. You feel a sense of accomplishment, but as time goes on, the fact you built a piece of furniture becomes irrelevant, and it's just another matter of fact in life. A more fulfilling goal is learning a new skill for life. That skill is always there, and from time to time, you enjoy the benefit of learning that skill and accomplishing that goal, and sometimes in life, you set a goal, and it becomes a skill.

Everything around you is based on two principles — choice and acceptance. Exceptional individuals either accept what is and build slowly, or they choose different paths and drive their desires and choices because they refuse to accept their current path, they have a hunger for more.

People who tend to follow a 'group think mantra' tend to indulge more in the principle of acceptance, but a more balanced exceptional mind uses a combination of both. You accept the current situation but create a series of short-term goals to build up to a change, and by their own choices and actions, they accomplish beautiful things.

Successful women in the business world understand the benefits and risks of group think opportunities in a fast-growing society that tends to push group think scenarios and models of business. A more casual term for this is trends. A woman with an exceptional mind may recognize the benefits of group think and take what they need from those scenarios and master a balanced level of success.

When people hear 'group think,' they often miss key elements in identifying there are some benefits but individualized creativity must be evitable in any group think scenario. Group think can often lead to an inability to change or take risks in presenting new ideology. In order to create change, an individual or business must be willing to make changes no matter how difficult or risky it can be.

Changes are uncomfortable in a business scenario or on an individual basis. Change now and again is necessary to maintain a consistent and optimal balance in the case of any operation of the business or individual goal.

A well-balanced woman recognizes self-care and the importance of hard work, change, goals and fulfillment. Not all change is bad. In fact, taking a risk by making changes has an endless list of benefits. A few of these benefits may include growth, knowledge and a more rewarding quality of life. One important detail of the actual execution of these changes is that you, as a leader or business owner have to be confident in these changes, and your execution plan should reflect the excitement.

A leader should be well-versed in these changes and ready to lead their own team with confidence and dedication. A leader knows change can be challenging for their team members, and patience is required during execution as well as persistence. I always remind leaders to be mindful that not everyone learns at the same pace and not everyone deals with changes the same way; some may struggle, and that's very normal.

As a leader, you should be able to identify which of your team members will require some additional support. Some of your team members may learn at a different pace and really need someone to assist them, and modeling that confidence and excitement usually will spark a fire inside your team.

An exceptional-minded individual is a great leader naturally and is quick to identify each team member's individual needs and will be quick to solve any bumps in the road early on and help transition a team the best they can.

Exceptional minds are usually well versed in what I call profiling the people around them and understanding in great depth the behavioural patterns and needs of the people around them.

Exceptional leaders are not people pleasers but rather carry a developed and balanced style in their approaches. They see each person around them in a resilient view always and recognize that they have their own attributes and strengths that are valuable and work towards building others up and using an equal exchange of power and integrity. They understand that every person around them brings forth unique talents and skills, and they build off those skills and attributes.

It's easy to fall into the trap of feeling resentment towards team members who may lack in certain areas or skills, but an exceptional-minded leader takes that information and uses it as an opportunity to speak and teach to their team individually in a language they understand. Sometimes we have to get the message we are trying to convey or the skill we seek to teach out and have to dig deep in the pockets of creativity. We must always be willing to work with others in a way they need and feel valued.

In order for everyone to be successful and on an even playing field, there has to be a consistent code of moral conduct the leader strives for and models. It is important we learn to work with others on an individual level and recognize differences are plenty, but together a lot can be accomplished.

Differences can be barriers when we are not aware that they exist; however, differences are truly a strength. Leaders recognize that cultural, language, religious or personal beliefs all play a factor in the development and should always be respected and adhered to, especially in a workplace setting.

Differences should also be viewed as strengths and opportunities. We have to do the footwork and make sure that we help everyone succeed and let our creativity flow when it comes to these barriers and be quick in identifying them. When we are quick to identify and find solutions, we all win, and the exceptional mind is excellent at doing this. An exceptional mind is observant and becomes easily bored when it sits idle. It usually has a need for perpetual learning, growth and accomplishment, and when these are not met, they become unhinged or flat-out bored.

There is a constant need to thrive, and they do their best work during chaotic peaks of life. An exceptionally minded individual needs to be challenged often, focused and busy. One of the biggest challenges I've found with this mindset is the idle periods. I often feel that I am wasting opportunity and time for myself. I am not utilizing my full potential when I have these feelings, I then start internalizing this as not doing enough.

For myself and others, sometimes action is needed because it lights a fire inside of us, and we become creative in our goals and what we want to achieve and keep motivated.

Some of my best ideas and work comes during the evening hours when I am alone and can just internalize the world around me without interruption. Sometimes that moment of idleness is needed to recharge or practise self-care, reflect and assess progress.

The world is so fast-paced, and we are doing things just to fill the moment; it can be compared to when we reply just to reply. An exceptional mind can recognize when a moment is just a moment or if it's been well planned and thought out.

An exceptional mind can be very powerful or break you internally if you do not understand yourself, your needs, and what is happening around you. I say this because when our needs aren't being met, we can internalize things and become self-destructive. Self-destruction is a very damaging mindset because one bad moment can make or break an opportunity, but the exceptional mind observes all around them and carefully plans and rides out the storms.

When the exceptionally minded share observations, it typically serves a purpose. It's either to empower, protect or help a person grow. It's like having a loaded hand in a poker game and bluffing your way through until it's time to clean house. Be selective about what you choose to share and when you choose to share things. The exceptional mind never lets knowledge control them. It's a balance between giving people the knowledge they need and understanding timing.

You can speak a thousand words to others, but if they are not ready for the message, they won't hear a single word. The exceptional mind recognizes the value of patience and waiting for the right moment. There is nothing worse than a foot-in-the-mouth situation.

It's human nature to be wrong and make mistakes with your observations; that's why you need to be patient and make sure what you're seeing is accurate. Life can be elusive, and mistakes will happen, but the exceptional mind owns its mistakes and does so with pride and is always accountable. When the time comes to do so great leaders use their own personal failures and mistakes as teachable moments rather than use them to destroy their inner peace and confidence.

This models to the world and people around us that we are just human, and the expectation from those around us becomes more achievable. Making mistakes is one of the best ways to learn as long as you internalize the lessons. You need to ask yourself why it did or did not work. What could I improve? What are the messages I need to take away from this opportunity? I say opportunity because it is a great opportunity for growth and reflection. When we take the time to go through our mistakes and internalize the results it's a stepping stone to perfect our next stage of success.

Many excellent leaders around the world have numerous stories of their learning processes, and most will share their struggles and mistakes to motivate, empower and inspire. It's important during the planning stage of any goal or operation to acknowledge that things won't always go as planned, and we, as exceptional-minded leaders must always have a backup plan and learn to navigate through the difficult times as well as the good times.

When our flight and fight response is activated, we have the ability to thrive more efficiently if we have already acknowledged that it may not work out perfectly this time, but it's a start in the right direction.

An exceptional mind requires you to own those mistakes and communicate to your team this knowledge and why it did not work and always accept suggestions and hear what others have to say and what they experienced. Within every person lays an inspiration you may not know you needed.

In life, you will meet many characters and personalities that can be unique, some amazing, and some you meet will test your character and personal skill set. The most meaningful moments will teach and inspire you and will test your strength and character to the core. The real test is whether you can manage the environment and team around you.

There will always be people who, for whatever reason, will cause you turmoil inside and around you; things they say or do will trigger you and perhaps others because you do not understand them or their rationale behind why or how they do things. There are always reasons; however, our job as an exceptional mind is to acknowledge our true feelings toward this individual or situation and ask ourselves how we are feeling about whatever the case may be and why.

The why will be the biggest factor in self-mastery because it's the first step in the foundation of understanding ourselves. We may not like someone or something because their actions trigger us, or maybe they remind us of a past experience, person or place. We may have had a past unpleasant or traumatic experience.

Perhaps we do not have the adaption skills or coping skills needed to respond to the elemental factors around us. Exceptional minds can become frustrated quickly with themselves because they know better in most circumstances but can often be ruled by emotions rather than rationale. This should always be avoided, but generally, overall awareness of this factor is considered during reflective periods. The most helpful approaches are to be genuine in your feelings and responses, admit when you are overreacting and take a break and come back to the scenario. Avoid being reactive and rather approach things with composure.

Emotional intelligence is often a rare character trait in many people today, but it's a skill that can be practised and mastered. The exceptional mind can begin to learn to use what I call level-four intellectual statements. These types of statements explain the why, acknowledge an emotion or action and are typically empathetic toward the audience. Here I will present a scenario and statement that gives a Level four response.

CASE EXAMPLE

Sally is in her 60s and often gardens every Saturday morning. Alison lives next door and has scheduled a roof repair that will be loud and disruptive to her neighbour. The statement below is an example of a proactive Level-four Emotional intelligence response.

Alison: Good morning Sally, I hope your Friday is going well. The reason for my visit is to let you know tomorrow morning; our roof repair guys will be doing some work on our roof. It will be loud and disruptive. I know how much you love gardening Saturday mornings. I apologize in advance to you. I wanted to give you a heads-up prior to the work being done.

Sally, flattered that her neighbour acknowledges her passion and the inconvenience, smiles and accepts the impending gloomy news. Sally will likely respond with a 'thank you' and be able to plan her Saturday around her needs, and a situation that could have been problematic is avoided. When we are proactive and recognize others' feelings and our own during any circumstance, we can clearly and strategically have better responses to the situations and people around us. Sometimes, in the moment, we do not respond the best, and these skills train your brain to have a sense of delayed gratification and slow down and provide statements, actions and responses that are more meaningful and help the people around us and ourselves.

A lot of the time, when we don't like something, there is always a chance that we may not have all the details; perhaps we don't understand all of the circumstances. This doesn't mean that we ignore our feelings or that they are not valid.

We must always honour our feelings and validate them within ourselves. A master of self internalizes, accepts and figures out strategies on how to better deal with circumstances or individuals that we don't like.

A key phrase that helps us remember this type of self-mastery is: Accept what is and let go of what was. This type of mindset is a more peaceful approach rather than negative self-talk. Overall emotional intelligence is a powerful tool to prepare the world and people around us for anticipated futuristic events and circumstances.

This level of intelligence thinks of others and is mindful of the interactions ahead, and avoids conflicts, miscommunications and problematic responses.

Chapter 2

THE CORRECT PERSONALITY

The personalities of the exceptionally minded are rather unique and often misunderstood by others who may not be self-developed themselves or may have personal struggles. Conflict seems to find us at times because we are very true to our feelings and genuine. This can make people uncomfortable. People often get uncomfortable with honesty and someone who is clear and self-actualized, especially when it comes to the delivery of messages.

As an exceptional-minded individual, we recognize when someone is engaging in a power struggle or transferences. When I talk about transference in my writings, I am referring to those situations where someone around is feeling a certain way and often tries to transfer their feelings onto the people around them. People around us may be in a bad mood or experiencing a problematic situation and seeking something emotionally.

When you encounter these types of people, you have got to 'brick wall' them but display an empathetic response as well to avoid defensiveness. This means you do not give them the typical response they're looking for, which in most cases is conflict. Instead, you recognize the power you hold comes from your own composure, and you hold your emotional stance and do not get defensive or take it personally.

Every day we interact with many people, and you can change the outcome and quality of those interactions by asking yourself what a person needs or wants from this interaction and questioning, what they are seeking in this moment. If it's unclear, they will always let you know. Pay attention to their body language and how they're holding their stance. Sometimes the easier route may be to just give in to avoid a massive blow up, and that's okay too. But do not make it a pattern. Giving in is a typical solution in newer relationship dynamics when we may not be able to predict a person's intent.

Internalize that moment and what was really happening and evaluate next time how you will respond to maintain a fair outcome. Giving in 100% is always saying yes, which will cause much inner turmoil because we are not being congruent with our own desires or feelings or what is right.

There is a societal misbelief that one must be happy and positive all the time for a better life; although the interactions we have around us are often more pleasant and fulfilling with this mindset, it's not always realistic or achievable. This is because everyone around us is experiencing an outside life and experiences that we may know nothing about.

Maybe your team members have suffered exceptional trauma or misfortune in life, mental health or developmental delays in certain areas of cognitive abilities. From experience working as a helping professional some of these variables can cripple one's cognitive abilities further and can often mirror other variables and can lead to distrust and damage to the relationship.

Someone you work with may be flighty and unreliable all of a sudden, and you as a leader notice this. Although its an inconvenience to a team and overall operations, as a leader you must always be cognizant and tread lightly when approaching performance because that team member may have something going on beyond the scenes that is heavy, and you, as a leader, want to show empathy and support. However, be clear and firm about what the expectations are when they show up. Acknowledge this before having the conversation because sometimes they are already on edge and in defence mode.

Certain language and tones may cause a blow-up. This doesn't mean you give in to them and allow unwanted behaviours, but it means you compromise. Whether it means that their duties can be modified, you give them more time in their personal life, or you offer them local resources. Sometimes our solutions must be creative and unique and adjusted to our team members on an individual basis.

Remember, not every team member or person around us can be painted with the same brush nor ruled by the same strategy. In order to get the best results from each person, we must always be willing to understand the huge differences in the people around us. This does not mean you give into a favouritism approach, but rather you compromise while adhering to your own expectations and theirs in a way that honours both parties' needs and obstacles. What is good for one is not good for all! This phrase will stick in your mind for a lifetime and offers a neutral stance and forces us to recognize that every person we encounter is riddled with individuality.

Being able to recognize personality differences and work with them in a way that honours both the leader and team member has the best outcome. We have all worked with toxic leaders at some point, and it can have everlasting effects on team members. Whether this be an old coach, manager or even a school principal, many have stories to tell. We will discuss later the effects of toxicity on a team and how to correct it and overcome the roadblocks and recover your team.

Be willing to compromise and, have the hard conversations, go into these scenarios without assumptions or judgments. Be willing to be versatile and creative when dealing with any conflict situations. Exceptional-minded individuals strive to have charming personalities that are fair, balanced and composed in nature.

The correct personality of an exceptional mind is always under construction and developing. People who strive to be exceptional are friendly, helpful and prepared. Most who can be identified with this mindset have great social skills, networking abilities and typically are creative and, very observant and self-aware. They lead with confidence for the most part and are always organized and goal-orientated with a strong desire and compassion fueling their motivation.

Exceptional minds are innovative and always quick to want to make positive changes to the world around them as well as being accountable overall. Exceptional leaders model behaviours that empower and offer opportunity for growth, learning and build leadership as a whole.

The correct personality for exceptional minds is a remarkable mindset that gives everyone something to seek, build and master to meet the needs of their team and people around them with a vision of success and celebration.

This mindset has challenges also but overall is a sure winning structure to help all leaders make their journey of success more fulfilling and inspiring to the world around them. Exceptional-minded leaders are not always born overnight, but with the right knowledge and persistence, it can be achieved for a captivating and bright future of success and change.

Chapter 3

TOXICITY RECOVERY

The first step of toxicity recovery is knowing that behaviour is a language and always has meaning. It is a very illusive language that can be decoded by careful observation, knowledge and awareness. It is a hidden language and often tells a bigger story about the person as a whole and their historical events and what is happening to them, and the experiences around them.

Disciplinary action isn't always the first solution you should ever run to as a leader however hearing their truth is and conducting your own investigation of what is being conveyed. Perception is everything. A behaviour may be hiding or mimicking something challenging for them, and sometimes giving someone a safe space, accommodations, knowledge, or motivational support is all they need.

You may even be able to have them own their behaviour, and if you're lucky enough, they may share bits and pieces of their story, and you may even understand the conflicts and situations a bit deeper and their unique character as well. You may gain a deeper knowledge of how to help them grow as a team member. There have been many moments I often wished I didn't open that can of worms because sometimes these conversations lead to dark places and discomfort.

As an exceptional-minded leader, you always want to shine that light into their world and help them grow. Every human you meet has a story and is a creature of habit, but in order to use the best methods and solutions available, you absolutely need to accurately assess and need to develop a sense of what and why it's happening and how to rectify the situation. It is necessary to use the best approaches to move forward and bring a sense of closure or solution.

In each person's life, there are always endless variables as to why they do the things they do. The why isn't ever the focus; it's the adaptation and measuring of whether they have the ability to bounce back after the incident or not and whether they are teachable. After a challenge, it's important for change to happen.

Understanding someone's flight or fight capacity is always a good observation as a leader to prevent future incidents or upheaval. Knowing if others are resilient and have the ability to own their poor behaviours and internalize the conflicts and situations so it doesn't keep popping up and disturbing the temperature of the environment around them is valuable.

In many of my own experiences, once one individual begins acting in a toxic or hostile manner, it often causes a domino effect on the people around them. Hostility and passive-aggressive behaviours are the most common triggers for people around you. Violence often causes immediate chemical reactions in the brain, and it's by no accident that this causes heightened behaviours and unpleasant moments around good teams. It sends human emotions into overdrive and can be a make-it-or-break-it moment for clusters of individuals.

If you observe a situation where this starts happening, you've got to deal with the main aggressors immediately because if you do not respond to this right away, the dominos start falling, and this will escalate into something that could have been avoided. You have to be comfortable with setting boundaries and being firm in what is acceptable and not acceptable.

After such incidents, you must always debrief the people around you and check in with them and not let leave them to debrief with other group members. The leader should always debrief because then it leaves no room for gossiping and potential advancement of toxicity.

You've got to teach them to make use of toxic situations, and you do that by identifying the unwanted situation or behaviour. Identifying how they felt about it in the moment and how it impacted them allows them to hear you as a leader and will avoid, protect and handle any situations in the future that are of a similar nature.

If you let it slide once, others will think this is normal and the standard within the team. Good leaders give their team healthy coping strategies, approaches and solutions that are more effective and benefit everyone as a whole. Good leaders respect comfort levels and team members' input. After toxic incidents, it can be deflating and create a loss of confidence. It can create insecurities and hyper-vigilant emotions and reactions. It can create fears and feelings of resentment.

A key indicator of huge turmoil within a team, business or organization is high turnover numbers among its members. This is the biggest indicator that can go unnoticed for periods of time, and by the time leaders catch it, it may be too late. When members start dropping off without reason, this is a clue that something is wrong and it's a good time to start asking questions and looking into what's going on.

Large turnover is bad for business. It is costly and word of mouth is powerful. One bad leader can cause irreparable damage and create a very bad reputation for a business or organization.

There will always be learning moments for every leader throughout their career; however, if this becomes a situation where they perpetuate this without accountability or any signs of growth, it may be beneficial to get rid of the leader or retrain because it isn't working in the best interest of morale, business and team needs. It is imperative to address the situation immediately and help all members recover and not sweep it under the rug.

Toxicity in a group setting can have detrimental impacts on an environment and create problems in the future. It can be a timely process and require a lot of patience but keep a positive mindset and combat toxicity and the aftermath with goals instead of gossip. Growth instead of blame and honesty instead of denial.

Accountability, without shifting of blame and apologies, makes everyone feel valued and heard. Focus daily on incorporating preventative measures for future leaders and encourage self-care and further skills development.

Some leaders may even introduce more prevention, policy, or rules to ensure and avoid future damage. Leaders who have opportunity to continue learning and further education and skills will always do better and strive for excellence. Have regular team meetings and provide opportunities for furthering skills., education and goals.

Leaders who have the chance to become goal orientated have less time to focus on negativity. Make sure training and skill set development is a priority and invest in your team. If teams feel they are learning and gaining new insights, they are more passionate about what they do.

When teams feel they know what they are doing and what they are trying to accomplish and are recognized for their hard work, they have less time to analyze toxicity and let it bring them down.

An exceptional leader offers praise, support, structure and teachable moments. Overall, the exceptional-minded leader can help a team make use of the aftermath of toxicity and empower their team to see through a new lens and view it in a way that is less damaging.

The leader who ignores toxicity as a whole may be setting the team up for it to happen again or face having resentful team members, and this could have detrimental effects on the overall operations and team. Never ignore what is happening or avoid it; strive to support and take preventative measures to avoid the aftermath of toxicity exposure and toxicity as a whole.

Toxicity overall is bad for business and has a huge influence on success and interpersonal relationships, and dynamics of the operation. Some leaders may not have all the skills they need to execute these types of scenarios or be prepared. It's imperative that all leaders guide and support these functions as it adds a protective barrier layer to all involved.

Working together is an important function when dealing with toxicity, as there can be legal ramifications if it is not approached in a proper manner. Exceptional leaders are mindful of their scope of practice and will seek support when it's necessary and never just assume.

Overall toxicity can really cause chaos and big problems and have detrimental effects; it should always be managed and assessed. Exceptional-minded leaders are always alert and aware of these factors.

Chapter 4

THE TOOL BOX

Success in life takes a mindset and commitment. Exceptional mindset leaders require tools, skills, and maintenance. Some of these helpful skills are self-discipline, self-celebration, self-determination, and self-actualization. These skills require constant work, assessment and progression reflection.

Many people tend to be overlooked in life in many contextual experiences unique to one's journey, whether it be jobs, promotions, love, finances, friendships or whatever it may be because of a few factors. You may be relying on someone else in life. I always tell people to stop waiting for that employer to notice their skills for a promotion or romantic interest to determine their success or even for that one loan company to approve them.

There are always opportunities everywhere. Sometimes you will have to be creative and put in more effort, but they exist, and your accomplishments can be limitless. Whenever something is too convenient or easy, there is usually a consequence, so always be alert and really think about all options.

Being open and acknowledging that you are not stuck is crucial. Your growth and success depend on this mind frame. Things can feel uncomfortable for a bit with change but knowing that change can be good and benefit you more is a valuable lesson as well.

Change can make the biggest impact on where you want to be in your life journey, and sometimes it's necessary. By viewing the world in a way that is positive, plentiful and prosperous, you begin to see through a new lens. As individuals, we hold the power to explore, seek and create wherever we go. This is what makes us such unique inhabitants of Earth.

We can change any outcome in a moment's time just by the choices we make, the encounters we have and by the physical actions we take. Exceptional-minded people know this, and they use it to better their lives and do whatever it takes to make life more satisfying and fulfilling.

Entrepreneurs often gain this mindset as they see everything around them as an opportunity to learn and progress. You have got to be a bit of a risk taker and trust yourself and your skill set. When we lack trust and confidence in ourselves, we begin to overthink and gaslight our own abilities. This mindset becomes toxic and sends us into a downward spiral of negative self-talk and emotional turmoil.

I have been there plenty of times. You've got to find your inspiration and what fuels your soul and focus on that. If it doesn't fuel your soul or make you better, shut it down, turn it off and regroup. A good way to determine what you want to do is to be sure to set goals and track progression and make self-commitments to execute where you want to be and explore any negative feelings that arise.

Do this by using a measurable progress-oriented goal timeline. One being a short-term and one being a mid-term goal. Take an inventory of how well you are progressing and the steps you need to take to get there. Think of how realistic your goals are and make a commitment to get them accomplished.

Exceptional-minded individuals are wonderful critical thinkers and have the ability to look at all angles of a scenario and sort through goals, tasks and situations and prioritize importance. These individuals can get things done quickly and effectively and push through difficult challenges and make use of all experiences, both good and bad.

Exceptional minds are passionate about achieving things and consume the knowledge around them. They understand the importance of the people around them and offer respect, authenticity and empowerment. Exceptional-minded people have an innate need to succeed and value self-growth and actualization; they are able to catch errors quickly and recover from unpleasant moments swiftly.

They have a wide understanding of the world around them and conceptualize risks and manage those risks accordingly. They end up creating opportunities and are very self-actualized individuals. These individuals are committed to growth and understanding the entire process of change and always have a backup plan.

You may find exceptional-minded people in all walks of life and in all sectors of work across the world. They offer balance and resilience and make excellent leaders and coaches. Of course, they may be really hard on themselves and very critical of their performance, but they eventually come to terms with who they are and their diverse needs.

Exceptional-minded individuals take on challenges and find solutions; they are not beaten down by complex equations of life that need solving. These individuals do not fixate on the troubled waters and make it the centre focus of their productivity. Most are creative and passion-driven.

I have found that they are exceptionally bright and talented when it comes to awareness in general and often make great companions and friends. Exceptionally minded individuals are very rare in a world like today; they do not make excuses but find solutions and avoid dwelling on failures.

They typically take the lessons presented to them and re-route the way they approach things going forward. The exceptionally minded usually have a ton of life experience and are open to sharing their experiences in a light that captures a motivational angle and inspires others who may feel hopeless. Exceptionally minded remind others that they have power and are the only ones who can make the changes they need to build healthier relationships, create life-changing opportunities, and achieve greater success for themselves.

They do not seek societal validation and are confident in who they are and are not driven by ego. Ego is a very difficult mindset to have. When ego runs a person, and they are ruled by their ego, it devalues the experiences around them. Ego is a protective barrier of the mind that only slows down a person's growth and hides the truths we may be uncomfortable growing from and being honest with ourselves about.

In a world where many face a giant battle of ego vs self, you will find that these exceptionally minded have come to terms with this battle and are not afraid to look in the mirror or sit alone with their thoughts. Exceptionally minded people find ways that are positive to silence the ego and fill the empty voids in their personal minds. Exceptionally minded do not follow trends and have a strong set of morals and values; they do not see the need to follow societal expectations and tend to be very creative and maintain a very high sense of composure.

These types of individuals do not need to brag or gloat about the things they accomplish because their success speaks loudly. They do not let poisons of the mind rule their choices or thought patterns, and they use their own skill sets to make it happen for themselves. Exceptionally minded are great problem solvers and have the ability to adapt to the environments around them, and they lead in a way that honours everyone around them.

These individuals do not let many things hold them back and often speak up to injustices and are not easily influenced by elemental forces. In the world, things are always moving so quickly and always changing, they may be reluctant to change at first, but as always, they adapt and change. The exceptional-minded love with their entire heart and take pride in the world around them.

I tend to notice exceptionally minded are drawn to the helping field and are often very nurturing and family-orientated. Of course, every individual has many traits and behaviours, but generally they share a lot of common traits listed and continue to grow and learn each day.

Something I've noticed is they have a higher sense of emotional intelligence and thrive when they feel supported and appreciated. They will make an effort to make changes and be consistent in all they do. Overall, they care very deeply about their well-being and work really hard at success.

Exceptional minds are not held back by barriers or issues that may arise; rather, they focus on solutions and generate new innovative ideas that empower the world around them. You may even see them taking on many projects or tasks and taking on excessive responsibility to keep their minds sharp and always busy.

I find they often are hyper-vigilant and have a need to stay focused. Not everyone is going to appreciate their presence because often people can become intimidated by their success and unique expressions of self, but that never stops them. People hate what they fear, a cold, hard truth of life. Fear is another mindset you will see absent from their list of traits, they have the desire to achieve, and fear is normally viewed as a barrier to them, and they do not let it steal their joy.

People may also view them as deep or very intelligent, and when others can't figure them out, they may assume who they are, and that may be frustrating for the exceptional-minded as they are usually pretty confident in who they are and have worked hard at the mastery of self.

Exceptionally minded spend a lot of time investing in their growth and development and always continue to educate themselves and are open to new ideas and views. Everyone of course, is different but these minds generally make excellent leaders, entrepreneurs, and business partners because they are so versatile. Exceptional minds never let the world around them get too dark and are always willing to be that change the people around them need. Exceptionally minded are always uncovering life-changing attributes about themselves and make self-revelations a priority in order to understand the world and people around them.

Exceptionally minded may possess some or all of these traits, but there are some negative traits too they have to overcome. I have found they include negative self-talk at times and huge self-disappointment when their goals or needs are not met. Sometimes exceptionally minded cannot understand the behaviours and lines of thinking around them at times and they can become very conflicted when they see prominent denial, deceptions, or bad practice in general.

Sometimes they may have so much passion or energy that it can really scare some off, and they can be misunderstood easily by others around them. These things never stop the exceptionally minded; they keep going and keep pushing to change the world around them. If you are one of these individuals or know one, they are a true measure of leadership and resilience.

They hold a diverse toolbox that contains some of the most high-end quality traits, and they know how to use them to make the world around them work. The difference between the exceptionally minded and the average mind is that no matter the pressure or struggles they come across, they maintain a healthy and balanced mind that rejects an oppressive and depressive state of mind.

They overpower and deflect struggle, problems and misfortunes and remain true to their integrity and values. No matter the lengths or life attempts to crush them under pressure, they remain with their grace intact and give meaning to their journey. They see the value and growth that can come from rough waters, and they learn while remaining true to an extraordinary act of strength and resilience. Exceptionally minded are truly gifted, and anyone can work at becoming exceptionally minded.

The exceptional mindset is achievable when we choose to observe through a new lens and embrace our unique character and shine light into the darkness around us rather than choose to sit in the dark and tear ourselves down. Life doesn't always go as planned and surely gives many lessons we didn't think we needed, but the beauty comes from finding an ounce of joy or happiness while growing and embracing the need to always learn, grow and laugh.

Being exceptionally minded is not only a state of mind and declaration of character for some but also a very wonderful goal to work toward. No one is born perfect, and our journey of life is always changing, but if we can make the slightest changes or great changes in our overall character and life as we experience it, we can change the world around us entirely by having more meaningful relationships and teaching others through our own behaviours and acts of character.

You have the tools to make yourself a stronger exceptional mind or even become one. It will take patience, self-reflection and accountability and a deeper understanding of self, but it will be worth it.

Chapter 5

Surrounded by the Great

There is a commonality most successful people have. The company they keep. A lot of successful people recognize the importance of being surrounded by like-minded people. It's not a mindset of being better or above anyone; it's the mind set about protecting your own energy and being able to be on an even playing field when it comes to business and having similar goals. It's the mindset of being inspired by people who have knowledge and skills that can help you build, create and share what has worked in the past and what hasn't.

Surround yourself with people who own their part of the story, the ones who recognize their own toxicity and are willing to tell the raw truth no matter how bad it looks. Someone who is confident in their own ability can own all the truths about who they are and use them to inspire others.

Exceptionally-minded people don't hide behind titles and positions in society. They may hold them, but their ego rarely gets in the way. They listen, observe and offer congruent respect to the people around them. Exceptionally-minded individuals hold a badge of integrity, and they use the strength they have to acknowledge the failures of all parties. No matter how defeated they feel, they dust their knees off and make a comeback and they choose not to let a fall define them.

They take all their wins and losses and learn. There will always be rocky bumps along the way and challenges, but they regroup and figure out what went wrong and strive to make a bigger comeback. They are the definition of resilience. Life is a giant game of cat and mouse and a triathlon of challenges on a daily basis that require a will of determination and patience. There will be choices where you get cold feet. We can choose to be fearful of making mistakes or embrace them and learn.

Life can be relentless and cruel, leaving us wondering what the point is of all the suffering we endure. The exceptionally minded recognize the danger of people who fuel toxicity. The most successful healing after any unpleasant experience is when we are honest with ourselves about what happened and want the people around us to reflect those attributes. We are able to have the hard conversations. We own our part that make us uncomfortable, and we feel all the emotions for what they are and accept what we can't change about whatever it is that has happened and keep going.

Surrounding ourselves with these individuals can help us grow and get through the tough moments. Exceptionally minded choose to surround themselves with individuals who are highly motivated and practise self-care regularly; they understand the importance of healthy boundaries and work hard to make things happen in their world. These types of successful people are usually organized and live very detailed routines that include a centre focus of balance.

Balance is crucial while striving for success. If we are working too much, it can lead to burnout, and burnout is costly. Burnout can cause others to act in a way that doesn't honour one's true character. An example is cynical behaviour, usually a trait of burnout, and these traits can be viewed as negative.

Leaders seeking success are quite self-aware and encourage the people around them to carry the same traits. They also admire accountability and respect those around them that are accountable. Leaders that aspire to be successful thrive on accomplishment and goals and should find like-minded people; otherwise, if the people around them are not making moves, it can be seen as bragging by the unmotivated.

The exceptionally minded value health and wellness and make it a priority to practise self-care and form habitual practices that honour that aspect of themselves. When leaders surround themselves with others who are striving for excellence, they can fuel one another and create new innovative ideas that are creative, challenging and success focused.

When leaders choose to surround themselves with others who are not doing much, certain behaviours tend to arise. These behaviours may look like gossip, jealousy, slander and putting down others. All very negative behaviours. It's very important to always surround yourself with people that are going somewhere and who inspire you.

All interpersonal relationships should maintain an equal exchange of power and mutual respect. When respect is not reciprocated, it can be frustrating, and it can cause resentment and really affect our mental health. You want to always make sure you surround your being in people, places and things that make you grow, feel good and inspire you.

A lot of successful people are really self-aware and have a good sense of who people are; they are quick to spot someone who doesn't have their best interests and don't let time or emotions rule whether or not the people around them are genuine. It never matters how long you have known someone because sometimes people trick us or mislead us into thinking they care or admire what we are doing, but their actions prove they don't.

When it comes to money, don't ever trust anyone, not even family, because some will take from you and never give. People can elude us using our emotions and vulnerability, leaving detrimental effects that can be costly and knock us down. Always be on guard and move in silence. When people become jealous or intimidated by someone's success, they can sabotage or do things to try and bring you down.

I have personally experienced many accounts of this and have been taken advantage of all too often. Always remember many are out for themselves, and if you give access to your world to the wrong people, they can turn it upside down, and quickly. When you surround yourself with good people who are focused on their own success, they won't have time to sabotage you.

Always be careful who you trust and never say anything to anyone you wouldn't say aloud around others or could not be accountable for. Humans are innately messengers; they have a need to talk and get their views out to the world, and with social media usage increasing and platforms being so accessible, we tend to see a ton of people engaging in smear campaigns and doxing.

Networking is crucial in building skills and businesses, and often, sectors and industries are pretty tight-knit and small. One bad incident can travel fast, and your side of the story may never be heard. It's very important, as exceptionally minded individuals, that you choose your supports, business partners and friends carefully.

Someone who doesn't celebrate your successes and clap for you likely isn't on your team. Exceptionally minded take note of the world around them but do not engage in retaliation or act on ego as a motive to negatively impact the world around them. Instead, they offer solutions and seek a deeper sense of self and development to enhance the relationships, environments and people around them.

It's acknowledging the world around them and their great influence. If people knew the power of who they are and how they can shape the world around them just by focusing on their inner growth and awareness as well as their own quality of interactions around them, they could begin to see what they can offer the world around them.

I think a lot of people are tired, they're distracted, and just generally overstimulated by the world, and some of those barriers can have an impact on others and their level of character commitment. The only thing we can control is ourselves to better advance the environment around us and make everlasting impacts on our world and the experiences we live through.

Sometimes we won't easily find exceptional-minded individuals around us, but we can strive to be one and influence others to achieve better ways of life.

Chapter 6

SURROUNDED BY TOXIC POSITIVITY

A lot of people always associate positivity as being a superior trait, and it can be when used in the correct context. Many times, in life, though, we see toxic positivity. Some individuals around us may not recognize it when they see it, and it's one of the worst forms of toxicity, whether it be in workplaces or interpersonal relationships.

What it looks like is an individual expressing a trauma, event, emotion or innate action and the other person generalizing it with a comment or expression with the culture of, "It could be worse, "or "It will get better." What happens is the person expressing that type of feeling around a circumstance minimizes the other's feelings as not being valid.

It deflates the other person of their life circumstance as it can leave them exiting a conversation feeling unsatisfied, unheard or guilty for their choice to share a very uneasy circumstance. Earlier, we discussed levels of emotional responses, and it comes down to being able to identify whether you're listening just to reply or you're really listening to the people around you.

People always reply with, "I am sorry this is happening to you," but often forget to validate what others are actually saying. When someone is going through a storm, they're usually seeking an array of things from others. Ask yourself, "What is this person seeking from me? What does this person need? What do they want or feel in this moment?"

When exceptionally-minded individuals do this before responding, they are getting into a healthy habit of exercising their level of emotional intelligence. The person with whom we are having these conversations, often leaves that scenario feeling you're more trustworthy, compassionate and a true leader with exceptional skills.

When leaders often dismiss what a team member is feeling and their needs, it leaves others feeling undermined and unsatisfied. It can lead to barriers and breakdowns in communication, transparency and trust.

Some of the most successful teams have a sense of trust in one another, and that's how they succeed together because they know they have one another's back. Teams are not just work-related. They are also for leisure; examples are sports teams, and sometimes families as well.

Teams are inclusive units and groups of trusting interpersonal relationships with the same goals and visions, morals, values and standards. Challenges with Positive toxicity-driven statements are that they are very passive statements that don't offer much context or substance. They offer minimal support, comfort, or knowledge. They are typically standard replies that we often hear in our day-to-day activities. They are not raw, honest or satisfying conversations.

Toxic positivity could also look like conversation derailment meaning the listener instantly cuts the conversation off and tries to control the narrative but makes it appear that they are present in the moment with you. It may look like they are controlling the tone while displaying a visible avoidance. To overcome an unequal balance in this type of situation, be firm in your points and hold them accountable in the conversation by addressing that tactic right away or stop talking to them, period, until they are more willing to really want to hear you.

Toxic positivity is also disguised sometimes as someone who plays the negotiator. The negotiator portrays that the conversation is okay to have with them, then begins with a tone that they care while questioning what you are saying and trying to tell you how to feel or how you should. They say that they just care and you're being negative and need to view it a different way.

Negotiators have a way of manipulating the facts you've stated and often leave the talkers feeling unheard and leave them questioning if their own feelings are valid.

Another tactic we often see is that positive toxicity is the competitor, although we understand the intent is often to assert empathy by using a similar experience that they have encountered. Sometimes the listener will often use their own experiences to make the talker feel their situation isn't so bad, or they often try to normalize what is happening to the other person.

Although most understand that this is a typical response, it can also be very toxic as we are derailing the talker from actually expressing how they legitimately feel, and important points may be missed because the talker is distracted and not actually expressing how they feel. This can also leave the talker feeling invalidated because their message is not being heard, and they can become frustrated very quickly. If they are frustrated, they may feel they are now taking on more negativity, negativity that is not helpful to their own recovery from traumatic events or experiences.

There is a big difference between saying, "I have dealt with a similar situation, and this is how I experienced it and how I handled it," or simply the other person using their own experience merely for the sake of responding or for their own emotional validation. It may indicate that a person still has not healed entirely from that situation and may make the talker less confident in sharing things with you again.

It is important that people trust us with their honest thoughts and experiences so we gain a better knowledge of what's taking place around us. When we have a deeper understanding of the people around us, we can have more meaningful experiences and improve the environment around us so that we have purpose and are goal orientated. Exceptional minded are present rather than distracted all the time, and they make others feel heard. These individuals give confirmation that what the other person is experiencing is valid. Exceptional minded offer support, resources and an ear to listen effectively.

When people feel they are not being heard or their struggles are a burden to someone else, they may never open up again and certainly not to the listener. When we validate another person, we hear their message. And, if we do so effectively, this person is likely to open up to us and come to us when something is happening to them in the future. Another way to effectively listen is to paraphrase what the talker is saying. Exceptional minded do this by paraphrasing what they are saying and using neutral statements like "Did I hear you correctly when you said this or that?"

When we are present for others, we are also present for ourselves, we are now slowing down in a fast-paced society, and we are showing up for people who need us the most. The rewards for being present in the moment are, more meaningful conversations, more meaningful relationships, more trust and more authenticity. It helps to build our leadership skills in general. Leaders have a duty to be great listeners and effective communicators; that is a big part of leadership because at the end of the day it is not always the tasks that you complete that make a difference, however, they do make a literal impact but can't always be the focus.

The biggest impact you'll make when leading a team is building a team that trusts you, that respects you and that you respect. A team that understands that you have their back will have your back, and an equal exchange of power occurs. When an equal exchange of power is prominent in a relationship, there is an absence of conflict and power struggles. A team who has a cohesive bond will always go the extra mile and work hard with you. Exceptional-minded people build cohesion by acknowledging that being a positive leader is important and have a need to step up and make sure that hearing team members' concerns is important. Exceptional leaders consider how their team might be feeling in difficult moments they are presented with. Team building where there is little to no support can leave a person feeling burnt out entirely, defeated and resentful.

Toxic leaders are everywhere; this is a reality, and striving to do better is what an exceptional leader recognizes. I am sure we have all witnessed or maybe experienced many toxic behaviours and watched participants be exposed to very toxic behaviours, including yelling, berating of competencies, intimidation, constant undermining, and embarrassment take place. This happens to many workers, and they begin to think this is a normal environment. They may even develop an unhealthy work ethic and leadership skills and bring them to other workplaces and environments themselves. The damage is often done and rooted deep within a group very quickly.

The recovery from toxicity exposure becomes the centre focus, and operations or overall thriving in a group setting can take a hit. High performers may lose confidence and be on guard. Your high performers may even move on to new places and experience burnout and high-stress levels. Team players may leave and develop unhealthy behaviours as a direct result. If there is no aftercare or conversation after toxicity exposure, the group may even feel resentful, and as a leader, you may even miss a crucial opportunity to have teachable moments and correct unwanted behaviours.

Leaders should address unwanted behaviours and correct them swiftly and quickly and help members move forward and support their team by having one-to-one conversations and regularly praising and rewarding positive behaviour and using positive verbiage. Aggression and unwanted tones can trigger past toxicity exposure and cause a team to relapse into old unwanted behaviours.

It is important things are not just swept under the rug because this can come across that you don't care as a leader, and they may feel unheard and undervalued. Avoid posting general memos in regard to toxicity exposure, and make it more personal. Apologise and redirect. Do not share intimate details about other members or performance details. If the conversation starts to become degrading towards other group members, then it's a good idea to derail that and bring it back to the person you are speaking to and create a plan to help them succeed. I have seen many toxic behaviours that can occur in a team setting, and it affects operations and each person significantly.

Some other manifestations of toxic behaviour are the silent treatment, yelling at others, starting intentional conflict, remarks or gestures that are degrading and embarrassing, creating hostile environments, and so much more. One of the worst toxic behaviours is slandering and gossiping about team members, which creates a hostile environment and decimates confidence and goals are no longer the focus. Turnover numbers become significant, and staffing shortages or member shortages become a huge issue. This, in turn, leads to huge emotional distress and burnout for everyone as well as huge costly training operations.

Toxicity is one of the most difficult processes to move forward from and bounce back from. With the right resources and care, any exceptional-minded leader can make excellent progress. Be sure to always document with follow-up emails after conversations and meetings. Always speak up, and never let a leader take advantage of you. Sometimes people will cause problems if given the chance and may get away with it because of fear of consequences from others. The workforce today can be a mess with the mental health pandemic rising.

As a leader, it's important to be familiar with regulations, policies, standards, and laws. Make sure you are up to date on all regulations and practices. If you are unsure, reach out to top leaders or mentors. Leaders should always have some level of care and make others' concerns a priority; leaders have a duty to protect others and their rights.

Sometimes terminating a bad apple doesn't always equate to a solution because the damage has been done, and it ripples down and creates a domino effect. The aftermath is always challenging to rebuild team cohesion and confidence again. It is imperative that if you are not experienced in handling complaints, challenges, problems or concerns, you utilize your resources and always have a witness present and record of some form.

Confidentiality is an important key factor. If staff begin gossiping about anything related to such issues, address it right away. Avoid engaging or sharing any other details with others. It's imperative you focus on the recovery process with your team and help them grow their skill sets and individual goals rather than focus on gossip. A common mistake leaders make is discussing others and issues with other members, and this only breeds further toxicity and re-exposes a team.

Conflict in a group is sometimes inevitable, but exceptional-minded leaders are quick to de-escalate it and defuse the situation. Leaders should always address it and correct it. Leaders should always model the behaviours they want their team to have and respect all members. Some leaders may even show leniency or favouritism to certain members, and this is not the type of behaviour or image you want your team to have about you.

Leaders recognize every team member is different and may require a different standard of care or method in how they approach and handle each member. Avoid mirroring favouritism. Consistency is the priority. If one is coached, then the other should be too. Exercise fairness and avoid extreme disciplinary action all the time. Sometimes it could be a matter of re-training or perhaps setting a clear boundary. Sometimes leaders are not liked because they are the ones that oversee everything; do not take it personally if it's a matter of doing the right thing, especially when enforcing policies or safety.

If you as a leader need to debrief, then reach out to your own leader and gain support that way. It's important to always protect the team values and your team members. This will help a group stay focused on the continuation of learning and growing. Own your personal mistakes and practise healthy self-care. Continue your own learning and growth, and stay committed. Be open and honest about your level of competency, and stay positive as much as you can.

Create a team that feels valued and always be fair. Being a leader is a continual learning process and a big responsibility, it has many perks and can be rewarding, but it can also have some downfalls. Always be open to feedback and criticism so you can continue to grow. Be sure to set regular goals and be exceptional.

The art of success depends on your willingness to be observant and identify risks and take preventative actions always. Success is a continual process and is relentless and full of challenges that require your determination and strength. It will not be an easy road to becoming an exceptional leader, but nothing easy is ever worth it. You have the power to change and shape the world around you.

Chapter 7

TAKING YOUR POWER BACK FOR EFFECTIVE LEADERSHIP

At some point in our lives we will experience a toxic workplace or toxic individuals and it can change us and our views on life. It can leave us with huge psychological effects and burn out. It can really overthrow our lives and cause a spiral of effects. For myself, it challenged me, defeated me, and forced me to grow. I didn't always handle it correctly because I became reactive after a long period of time and wasn't always handling it correctly. It's a good test of character. It doesn't define your character but often your level of experience and where leaders need to grow.

Workplace toxicity is a huge problem in the workforce and causes many to pick up unhealthy behaviours. I remember it started to affect my health. I became overly emotional, depressed and it left me questioning my skill sets and my own self-worth. In the moment, I couldn't see it wasn't me as a person; it was just the way I choose to respond.

Of course, Human Resource departments are always available, but workers should always tread lightly as Human Resource departments are there to protect an employer's business and will do so at all costs. A simple complaint can turn into performance reviews and plans leading to termination. It's costly for employers to pay out settlements and claims. It can turn into a 'he said, she said' game and most of the time, it's cheaper for an employer to find cause and terminate an employee. When an employer all of a sudden wants to discuss performance, be prepared and make sure to always have a paper trail. Have an employer recap everything in emails so you have that in case there is a claim later on. As a leader, be sure to always keep learning and participate in workshops that empower and keep you motivated. If you can seize an opportunity to develop skill sets, take them.

For me, keeping a log of my days and the challenges that arose and how I handled things was always helpful. If you notice you are experiencing a lot of issues leading a team, talk to neutral parties outside the workplace and explore what is happening with trusted sources. If you notice you are burnt out and not handling things well, take breaks or time off. Your health and well-being are a priority, especially since your team looks to you for support and leadership.

Good leaders are typically self-aware and can set personal goals for themselves, their team and general operations. A leader with no goals and no vision can be quick to lose sight of goals and get caught up in details that don't really matter. Another common mistake leaders make is oversharing their lives or personal details about their lives or themselves.

I've seen leaders cross boundaries with team members, and in return, respect is lost, and they are not taken seriously. It can create windows for gossip and unhealthy boundaries. Team members are not your friends or family. They are there to do a job and so are leaders. Model the behaviours you want your team to have always.

I've seen romantic relationships and friendships turn a team environment upside down. Avoid this at all costs. Silence is golden, and refrain from sharing anything with anyone. I also made past mistakes in sharing medical details with employers. I would caution against this also, especially cognitive-related issues or mental health-related issues. It can be used against you if you want to get a promotion or keep your position.

Sometimes people do not understand the medical world, or its implications and they may view you as incompetent or a liability. They may question your capabilities or foresee benefit pay outs of some type. Use discernment if you choose to share any medical details, and always keep a record of anything shared. In order to be successful, you have to keep a good set of boundaries and remember that you can overcome any challenge. Always plan ahead and keep organized. Keep documentation of any challenges and take opportunities to grow and learn. Sometimes we can't control what is happening in our world and the only thing we can control is the way we respond to it. That's how you take your power back.

Stay true to your morals, values and character and no matter the situation, you will learn and grow from it. A lot of people benefit from setting healthy boundaries ahead of time when entering any interpersonal relationship. Exceptional-minded leaders make a point if analyzing what they want from that relationship ahead of time, and they determine these boundaries by the type of relationship it is. They recognize the dangers of crossing boundaries and always maintain them accordingly. Sometimes individuals can get too comfortable with the people around them, and it can be detrimental. Any leader should consider the risks associated with a lack of boundaries and be clear and firm about what they are because others who do not see a clear visible line about what they are may cross them for their own personal gain or to take advantage.

There is an old saying, "The people who get upset about you setting those boundaries are the ones who likely need them the most." Most younger team members have fewer life experiences and really need to have those behaviours modelled for them because they likely have not been exposed to professional boundaries.

In my own work experience, I have seen many professionals be in ethical dilemmas as a result of poor boundary setting and it can cause a lot of issues. Most professionals are regulated by specific boards or ethics commissions, and even in the grey areas, if harm has been done as a result of lack of boundaries, it can cause trouble for well-versed professionals. If you are not sure, always have these conversations with more experienced leaders around you.

Exceptional minded, do not lead with emotions in decision making; rather they lead with a sense of professionalism and ration. As professionals, its very important to avoid emotional attachments and attachments in general to other team members. You can care and still be a great leader but investing too many emotional feelings into scenarios can lead to the unintentional crossing of boundaries.

Sometimes you will have to be vocal about what they look like because many in life often do not learn about them until later on in life. When professionals become too emotionally invested, processes of counter-transference and projection are more likely to occur, and exceptional-minded leaders want to evade this potential risk. There are many great ways to build rapport with people around us that do not include boundary crossing and too much personal disclosure.

Great ways to build rapport are focusing on the goals and tasks and using encouragement, praise and offering learning strategies. Of course, it's okay to make small talk but stay within healthy limits. Avoid subjects like political stances, religion, and personal trauma as topics. This can cause conflict, and sometimes, if we really do not know certain details, it can appear in a certain unfavourable light.

Exceptional-minded leaders often have experience working with others who have a great sense of humour, and in workplace settings, this can be problematic. Sometimes many will not find certain things funny and be offended, and this happens a lot. Everyone's level of acceptable humour varies from person to person, and even though some find things funny, for others, it can be offensive and triggering. Humour is a great characteristic in a person but should be used in acceptable contexts. You may even see other team members joke around and have fun, and it's not that you have to be a party pooper, but leaders keep a close ear on the context and can redirect the topic if jokes are inappropriate. In the food service industry, it's referred to as floor talk, and customers and others are always listening. Most complaints in a business are usually around how staff behave and conduct themselves. Complaints can be avoided if we encourage team members to use acceptable tones and control the context within earshot of guests and customers.

We live in a society that can be easily offended; guests have high expectations of customer service workers, and with good reason. If members are too focused on conversations they are having with one another, then guests can feel ignored and unsatisfied, and mistakes are more likely to happen if others are distracted.

Exceptional-minded leaders recognize the dangers of distractions. Distractions can cause an array of issues, especially when working with customers and in within a team setting. Distractions are normal on some scale because we all have a brain that never stops thinking and dreaming. When it starts to slow down service, accuracy, and takes away from learning opportunities, it starts to create a mediocre environment that others are not enjoying. It can become problematic. It can cause the loss of vision and goals as well as create windows of opportunity for gossip.

An exceptional-minded leader can keep distractions minimal and focus on tasks of importance and delivering excellent service. Technology can be a huge distraction in everyday living and relationships around us. Many people have experienced this type of distraction, either on a romantic level or interpersonal level. There is likely someone around you that is always on their phone or computer. Exceptional minds recognize the dangers of this element specifically. It can lead to a disassociation of the world around us, and the people around us might feel excluded or invalidated if this is happening often.

As exceptional leaders, we should strive to offer balance and eliminate major distractions, especially if we are carrying out tasks, services and listening to others. Distractions can also lead us to miss important details that are happening around us. When we are distracted, we may not be able to assess potential conflicts and risks around us. It's more likely miscommunications can occur when we are not focused on what we are doing or saying as well.

In order to take your power back as a leader after any situation, you must be on your best game. Taking our power back does not mean we engage in ego battles or power struggles. It is not that we are above anyone or devaluing others, but rather we have acknowledged our mistakes, loss of control or failures, and we bounce back as leaders to ensure we are carrying the exceptional mindset. Leaders take their power back by being honest, accepting accountability and assessing what went wrong and how we can improve the next time. Leaders make an effort to regroup, plan and execute smoother operations or tasks. Leaders avoid distractions and falling back into old patterns or behaviours we know that didn't work.

Exceptional leaders have a drive that is empowering, motivating and inspiring. Exceptional leaders recognize the importance of self-care, balance and pride themselves on their morals and values. Exceptional minds are always assessing risks, potential conflicts and ensuring there is no room for healthy boundaries to be crossed. Leaders carry out their tasks with positive mindsets and make a conscious effort to combat toxicity and provide environments that promote learning, teaching and self-development as a priority. These leaders take their power back after any misfortune by being cognisant of the world around them and how it directly interacts with and affects them. It can be challenging after any breakdown or event that may affect a team to bounce back but with careful thought processes and planning. Taking our power back can be done more effectively when leaders model the behaviours, effectively listen, take and make opportunities for growth and are attentive to the environment around them.

Exceptional minds are pro-active and organized and never miss a moment to do their very best and offer innovative solutions and ideas to advance their teams and the people around them. Exceptional-minded individuals are committed to making lasting changes that offer the most valuable moments for successful accomplishments.

Chapter 8

Underdog Revealed

One thing I've learned as a leader is how important it is to be hands-on. If you're leading any business, you should be where your team is so you can observe team members. It is crucial in developing a team and understanding how each member learns, their strengths and areas for development.

I've seen a lot of leaders become too fixated in offices and focused on operations and forget the business is still running and team members still have needs, such as guidance and opportunity to grow their skill sets. A wonderful and exceptional-minded leader is able to delegate effectively. The exceptional-minded leader understands the importance of teachable moments and takes their team members seriously and helps them grow within goals as well as celebrate milestones of achievement.

Exceptional minds recognize the value in each person in their lives and help others excel. They voice and compliment others and share everyone's success. Exceptional-minded leaders empower others by giving them opportunity and seeing each member's resilience, strengths and help identify areas where they can improve.

Exceptional leaders do not see weakness as a negative thing, but they help the member to improve, and they view it as an area they can help with and empower the member to gain skills, and they invest in their potential. The leader can speak in language that is clear, effective and motivational rather than punitive.

A common mistake leaders often make is disciplining members for not making operational goals by using anger, yelling, berating of others, personal judgements, intimidation or punishment. This is not effective. It can make matters worse and create hostility and loss of confidence as well as more conflict. A leader should observe closely and look for ways to teach in a manner that the member can learn from. There are many barriers to teaching. It's important to be mindful of them.

Everyone learns differently and at a different pace; be patient with all team members. Sometimes a leader may have to be creative. Great ways to teach are by using a variety of examples such as demonstrations, pictures, written steps, interactive programs, PowerPoint presentations, charts, graphs, and presentations. Many other types of strategies are available in various formats and languages. A lot of leaders even create specific presentation content and share it in-house. Regular group meetings help get the same message and content out to everyone, and it's more likely to be remembered and be a positive opportunity to empower others and have them be together to generate excitement and understanding.

This type of format also helps leaders observe the entire team's dynamics. Sometimes while working in a team setting, you may observe a team member and try to understand where the underperformance originates from and help them work on it. This kind of coaching is likely more effective for individual team goals. I found in my own life experience, during my studies in Child and Youth treatment while working an internship assisting teachers in the classroom, each student had their own barriers while learning.

Sometimes it could be mental health, cognitive disorders, cultural differences, memory recall, attention capacity and an entire array of other barriers. If you are not aware of the barriers, you can ask general questions of members to see what they are experiencing while trying to learn and work together to enhance those skills. An example might be the lighting may be too low if you see a team member squinting.

An exceptional leader should avoid asking medical questions or anything too personal; it could lead to serious ramifications, but an open-ended question that is directed at assisting someone in learning what works for them is important. You will have a very diverse group of people when leading a team, each with their needs, goals and personality.

One thing I found as a young entrepreneur is never to assume anything about anyone or dismiss another's ideas or capacity. Every being is valuable and important. When you view the world by what you know for a fact instead of what you assume, it is truly a helpful lens. A lot of individuals may even experience untrue thoughts about themselves that affect their self-esteem.

You combat false unhealthy thinking patterns with empirical evidence and knowledge. If someone makes an untrue statement about their performance or difficult task, you may say that you have never seen that in them, and they did a great job. Always redirect negative statements by highlighting where they excel instead and offer to help them grow in that area. Sometimes you will encounter an underdog, someone who surprised you with their performance and all they needed was a chance to shine or just a little bit of notice.

There is always one on every team. I have found they often just need to be identified and invested in. You would be surprised how many wonderful, skilled people go un-noticed and undervalued, and in return, they end up going somewhere else. This is why it's advisable to spend time with your team and understand each member and their impact and contributions.

Sometimes you may even see toxic leaders praised and invested in and put on a pedestal, while the ones who do a great job are often assumed to be doing mediocre work. This usually happens when the toxic leader feels intimidated and wants to take the heat off themselves. These types of leaders feel threatened by someone who outperforms them, and they typically make them feel small, create false narratives and throw them under the bus. That is a significant statement for a team. Nothing makes other team members want to run for the hills like that kind of treatment.

Watching not-so-great team members be praised for toxicity is very damaging and leads to resentment and huge turnover. As mentioned, consistency should be crucial in developing a team; avoid rewarding toxic behaviour, condoning or turning a blind eye to it. Exceptional leaders are able to redirect poor behaviour and treatment around them by setting boundaries, speaking up and documenting incidents.

Expressing individual favouritism towards certain team members can be misconstrued and create opportunity for gossip, it can be toxic as it creates comfort in a lack of boundaries. A good rule of thought is to lead with an equal hand. Your team members are always listening, watching and taking in each interaction, no matter if it seems they are distracted. They always notice. Praise and acknowledge each individual, and when targets or goals are met, celebrate everyone and their unique contributions and hard work.

Exceptional leaders should have a quick eye when it comes to identifying underdogs and problematic members and making necessary changes. Sometimes all an underdog needs to become a top performer is one person to believe in them.

Chapter 9

KNOWLEDGE & EMOTION

To be an exceptional mind requires individuals to have a sense of control over their knowledge and get familiar with how they use, view and retain knowledge as well as information. The exceptional mind uses information to enrich the environment around them, not just themselves. It's important that leaders of the exceptional mindset help others around them make use of the information that is correct as well as truthful.

Incorrect delivery of new information such as training material, policies, changes or goals of the business, is a danger. If a leader delivers the information in a negative, aggressive or overly punitive manner, it can cause a ripple of negative emotions through a team. Exceptional-minded leaders deliver new content in a positive way, that shows they are knowledgeable and truthful. The delivery of new information and execution of change can bring challenges and different behaviours. An example may be a change to policy that doesn't benefit staff or new mandatory training.

You can expect different reactions and emotions from staff and perhaps even some resistance to the new changes. Exceptional leaders help transition the team through the challenge and try to eliminate conflict by using their own responses and attitudes towards delivery or execution phases of delivery. Fear is common with any change, and leaders can combat that by using knowledge, and a positive mindset, highlighting any benefits and explaining the process of change.

Another aspect of knowledge and emotion that is often missed is the ability to analyze what went wrong with your team when you did not meet target goals. One time I asked a team what they thought happened when we missed our targets that day. It was an opportunity for reflection, and for the team to generate what went sideways and to collectively analyze how we could make it work, at least, that was the intention. Instead of the team shooting ideas, they went silent and took it as me being punitive to the point I got a message from another leader at home saying to blame her.

It was not the answer or intent I was looking for. I realized in that moment the team was running on emotion rather than knowledge and wasn't ready to analyze any information or knowledge. A team should always be prepared to look critically at any scenario without feeling offended. A lot of the time, people can become offensive when confronting mistakes or mishaps. This is a sign likely many are running on ego and emotions rather than knowledge or perhaps the team has developed a fear of discipline from other leaders.

Exceptional minds create an environment where people can talk openly about what occurred, and they encourage the team to generate new innovative ideas to succeed. It's never about blame and focusing on the fall. It's more about how can we meet our targets and goals. People who are offended by everything will struggle to achieve anything.

Emotional attachments to goals and targets may prevent many from genuinely looking at the whole picture. Most importantly, celebrate every step to success and be sure to praise and acknowledge what went right and continue to build on that. A lot of people really run on emotions and their ego, and some may not even realize they are doing so. It can prevent a team from even generating ideas or correcting what went wrong because they can become fixated on defence and offence. The goal should be to empower the team or group and build off of strengths and what worked.

I've learned not to take anything personally and to keep working on the strategies that fuel success and pave the way for success. Emotions can be very powerful, and many can get stuck on the emotional component of any goal, and emotions tend to cloud our brains. We are less likely to analyze a situation with knowledge and critical thoughts if we are stuck on an emotional attachment. The best approach is to acknowledge the emotion and figure out where that emotion stems from and put it aside for later. The only emotion you really need is compassion. You have got to love what you do and be passionate about it in order to strive for the best moments of success.

Overall, the exceptional mind recognizes the danger in the ego and letting it take over run your mind. Once you master control of your ego you become a well-versed individual, one who can silence emotions. The ego becomes a master of self rather than a slave to their own mind. A leader who has conquered the pending dangers of the mind becomes an incredible force when put into a team setting. You teach others how to lead, that is true, but you also teach others a set of morals and values and teach them how to conquer any obstacle, and together you create a flow that cannot be disrupted by elemental forces. You create a bond with individuals, and together you grow and can conquer any set of targets or goals. It takes time and patience and is relentless because there will always be new challenges and situations, but a leader of the exceptional mind status teaches from knowledge rather than ego and finds solutions rather than let emotions defeat them.

Lead with knowledge and genuine passion, and you will accomplish so much in a short period of time. People always have baggage and life stressors, but a lot of time, when we are really bothered by things happening around us, we really have to analyze why we have such an emotional attachment to those things and strategically combat those stressors.

Exceptional minds see a situation, make the assessments needed to move forward and make rational strategies that honour their team and goals without their ego or emotions, which can poison the process. That is the exceptional mindset that is needed for success. There will be times, however, when some of your top performers may struggle and present challenging behaviours or attitudes. As a leader, you want to explore that a bit deeper and find out what is happening for that team member.

If we choose as a leader to ignore it, be sure it will come back later on and create a disruption of flow later on. Exceptional leaders have to be good at managing people. Have those hard conversations and address the issues head-on. Your team's well-being and overall behaviours influence the environment, and a exceptional leader recognizes this. Sometimes you will have to deal with emotions and behaviours as it will affect overall success.

We have to present ourselves as a character with many hats. This means that sometimes we have to offer comfort, empathy and understanding. We as leaders do not just offer task-orientated training, but we offer life coaching as well. To be a leader means we make sacrifices and what we sacrifice is our feelings towards a situation to help others solve their own issues and work through their stressors and offer healthier strategies that motivate, inspire and empower others around us.

We empower the team to find solutions and help them with whatever is presented. In order to help others, we have to have an element of self-awareness and honesty with ourselves. When we fail at handling a problematic situation, it's crucial we own that, and we tell them what happened for us and why as a leader, in that moment, we couldn't meet their needs. Your team will respect you more for owning your failures, and it shows them you are not running on autopilot, and you are human as well and don't have all the answers all the time.

It's okay to make mistakes as a leader, but you have got to work hard to conquer those mistakes and plan ahead so you can make sure to avoid repeating them. The hardest thing you will ever have to do is swallow your pride and own when you are wrong, but your team will thank you later. Most people don't quit opportunities; they quit leaders, and if you keep that in mind, it's a good way to gauge whether you're doing a good job. Keeping our own emotions in check is a very difficult task on its own and requires a level of self-dialogue that is consistent and honest.

The mind is a powerful place, and every relationship and all content we fill our minds with has an impact on us mentally. Having someone say to you, "Just be positive," is not going to get you through that moment. I once had an employer tell me to be more positive. I felt invalidated and felt like this person made a poor choice in how they handled it, this individual didn't explore what was happening and missed a huge issue that was affecting the entire environment.

When we skip over the probing questions and caring enough to explore what is happening within the big picture, it can have serious consequences. As a leader, do not avoid conversations because they are difficult or you don't have time. Find time. You should make a great effort to find out what is happening and make sure you take proper steps and address it and take corrective actions. If you wait too long, it can have serious repercussions. The most toxic leaders do not hear their team or value other's input and try to micro-manage everything around them. Trust your team and hear them. They matter just as much as anything else.

Exceptional leaders can get things done and understand operations, but they also have the ability to manage the people around them. We manage people around us by caring and hearing them and striving to make a difference for them. Showing up physically is sometimes not enough but being present cognitively as well is what is required. When we show up, we are present and we offer a non punitive environment and make sure we keep a balanced environment. Exceptional leaders do not engage in the minimization of other's skills and abilities; they build off their strengths and do not compare their team members or let personal knowledge or emotion control how they treat others.

Sometimes we are wrong about the people around us because we do not have all the facts, and assuming only leads to problematic occurrences. Exceptional leaders should avoid assuming tasks are easy for everyone and having the behaviours of a know-it-all attitude and comparing their performance to others and using phrases like "They don't act this way for me, or do that to me," when speaking with other leaders. Instead, an exceptional leader will explore what was happening during the occurrence and offer support and get to the bottom of what happened.

Of course, team members will act differently towards other leaders for various reasons. When we compare and invalidate other leaders, we only lead on the assumption that the other leader lacks or is incompetent and in return, the issues never get resolved, and a teachable moment is lost. You may minimize other leader's esteem and, in return, make them feel they aren't doing a good job, when it just may be an issue of new challenges that arose during that day.

Exceptional leaders see the value and knowledge every team member brings to the table. It's not a competition, and leaders who have to be the best all the time create an environment where they are the best and no one can do a better job end up creating a toxic setting.

People will not respect them because they will always feel inadequate and will likely shut you out because they do not feel they can learn from you. These kinds of behaviours are often ego-fueled and scream that they need constant validation. Teach others without expectation and celebrate every milestone and success. Exceptional leaders value their team and work together collectively to make all things possible.

Chapter 10

UNDERSTANDING YOUR ROLE

Whenever you find yourself in a leadership role or team lead role it's imperative you understand what your role is and what tasks, goals and targets need to be met. Always ask questions and get a file or printout of what it is you are required to do. Always clarify if you do not understand or are unsure. From my own experiences, I have seen leaders just be thrown in without that knowledge, and they flop and fail. Whether it be lack of training, lack of initiative or lack of knowledge, you want to take accountability and be sure to become knowledgeable about what your role is.

Understand the daily tasks, operations and routines. Become versed with regulations in your employment sector or team environment and really look into these circumstances in great detail. In order to do a good job, you really have to understand your job. I have experienced many toxic situations where the person who was supposed to train me didn't really want to or refused to do so.

Sometimes other team members won't be happy you are coming onboard or are there for various reasons but one common reason is a company may choose to hire externally rather than give a promotion in house. When a company or organization does that, it means that likely the current leader has not trained well enough or prepared to advance any team members which is something you want to avoid as an exceptional leader. It's important as a leader you develop your team's skills and take the time to make sure if something goes sideways or is not jiving, someone else knows how to help keep the flow of the operations smooth.

It can also mean the top leader is seeking specific skills or experience that perhaps the current team would benefit from and is needed in order to further develop the team. Often other team members may push back a bit when you first get into a leadership role. They may test your boundaries and who you are as an individual. People fear what they do not know or understand. When people are ruled by fear of the process or changes, resistance can occur, and it can be challenging for new leaders. Do not take it personally and be sure you try to build healthy rapport and be open and honest with your mentor. If you understand your role and duties, you can learn a routine and really do a great job if it is clear what the rules, policies, goals, targets and expectations are.

Never assume what they are because of past experiences because every opportunity is a unique dynamic and has its own order of operations. Gather in-house resources, look at current manuals and training manuals and get knowledgeable. Also, always allow for a period of observation unless you see something that needs to be addressed, like health and safety liabilities, right away. Observation is important in understanding your role and taking in a new or changed environment because an exceptional leader avoids stepping on toes, engaging in power struggles and understands the power of observation. Observation gives a non-biased look into what is taking place, what is missing and what needs to be improved.

An exceptional-minded leader should avoid coming in, and making too many changes too quickly, which can cause chaos. This may even result in high turnover and may pose a risk of a hostile or toxic work culture. Keep records of observations and ideas you would like to change and set some personal goals based on your observations. Understanding your role can prevent you from being taken advantage of and having an increased workload without the title and pay. All too often, big organizations will do this to save a few dollars. I want to remind you, you should be compensated and recognized for your hard work. A lot of organizations will usually negotiate pay raises and promotions if you are able to successfully demonstrate what you have achieved and the things you have completed as an exceptional mind. Take notes and mark your progress each day. Documentation is key. Often, poor employers who want team members out can introduce PIPs which is a performance improvement plan.

Typically, when an employer introduces you to one, this is not a good sign. Those documentation records and notes will come in handy, and understanding your role is crucial. A lot of time, when your wage becomes costly and the benefits you receive become expensive to an employer, they may seek ways to cut those expenses out. It's very rare to have an employer who appreciates your hard work. Always protect yourself. Exceptional-minded leaders recognize how the economy and inflation impact operations as a whole. It can mean big budget cuts and wage freezes as well as lay offs.

Successful people are able to recognize they have to bring to the table a skill that no one else can perform. The world is competitive, and so is the employment world. It's crucial in developing yourself and your skill sets to be aware that toxic people exist everywhere and to be very careful about who and what you vent about. I would encourage having outside work support and not getting into unhealthy behaviours with co-workers. When you are successful and doing well, and it's being noticed, do not be surprised when others try to disturb that flow or peace. Jealousy and envy can occur on any team, and it's important to recognize that and protect yourself from very toxic power plays by others.

When I first started managing, I experienced this firsthand. I learned co-workers are not your friends and will do whatever it takes to make you look incompetent to make themselves look like they are outperforming you or anyone else. I had one co-worker who often would sabotage my efforts and try to undermine my goals and plans in front of top leaders. This co-worker befriended me and would engage in toxic patterns and try and make me seem incompetent. This co-worker had an inferior attitude and would degrade others to make it seem like she was the top dog. Of course, top leaders often see through these types of power plays. There is that old saying that blowing out someone else's candles won't make yours any brighter for a reason. For a long time I let this person whisper in my ear and it destroyed my confidence and my perception of what was happening around me. I kept going and eventually tuned this person out and their toxic behaviours.

Stay focused on your duties and tasks. Avoid getting so personally involved with co-workers that you lose sight of what you're trying to accomplish. Overall, your knowledge of your role is important, and the future of your success depends on the exceptional-minded individuals working hard to achieve goals and targets in hopes of improving the overall operations, and you cannot do that alone.

Build your team, focus on what each member brings to the table and help them find their inner motivation. Sometimes you will have to train yourself and be mindful of everything occurring around you and keep extensive documentation.

Each team will have unique needs and areas of improvement to succeed. Remember, no role will ever be the same and each comes with its own set of challenges, but let it be known it's an opportunity to build your skills and learn new ones. Time and patience are key in making changes and becoming an exceptional-minded leader.

Chapter 11

THE THIEVES OF SUCCESS

A lot of people often measure success by being a top earner or having a position of power, but I don't think that defines success at all. I've seen many successful individuals who were not at the top position or top earners outperform others.

In fact, the most effective leaders were in middle management, by my own experience. I have a feeling it's because they still had the motivation to get to the top and were hungry for success.

Often the leaders at the top forget what it's like to be at the bottom and let their egos get in the way a lot. There are some really good leaders out there at the top, but I have found that those middle-median leaders, have a lot of drive and compassion to get to the top. I have found in many industries, it's not what you know, it's who you know, and many franchises are still using older models based on nepotism and seniority. Seniority doesn't always equate to knowledge or the ability to manage people and everyday operations.

There are so many people who would do a great job and be more effective because they have no personal attachment to a business; they just run off passion and what's best for the entire business and team.

I have had the experience of working in family-based businesses and there tends to be a lot of conflict and conversations that take place in the background. If you get the wrong leader in there, it can turn a place upside down.

In every successful leader lay some thieves that can steal your ability to do your best. Burnout is a top one as it affects an individual deeply and presents various behaviours and symptoms that affect the entire environment. Exceptional minds are always assessing their level of functioning and are in tune with their feelings and what they are experiencing.

Exceptional minds can gauge when they have reached their capacity and workload and can effectively use time management, self-care and self-awareness as a superpower and make sure they are in good shape to lead.

Another common thief of success is envy or jealousy; this can often happen, especially when the expectations and wages are not consistent across the board. It can turn good leaders into very resentful beings and create a lot of chaos and conflict.

Some environments have clauses in their policies to avoid this type of disclosure; however, in other places in the world, this can be considered a violation. To avoid this, maintain consistency and combat jealousy and envy by exploring it on an individual level and understanding why that member may feel that way and try to diffuse that type of scenario by really listening and offering solutions that are fair and complement that individual.

Another thief of success is time management. Some leaders may have unrealistic timelines, or maybe they do not utilize the time they are provided. Exceptional minds are very practical and manage their time effectively because they recognize that not doing so can have terrible outcomes and can really affect the overall mission and goals of accomplishment.

Sometimes we can also see leaders leading with ego and emotions, which has already been discussed several times and also has another huge impact on success theft.

Leaders may often practise outside their scope and cause more damage as well. Be sure to do what you have the knowledge to do and reach out for additional support when necessary to avoid creating problematic situations.

There are many thieves of success in day-to-day leadership, but an exceptional leader always recognizes when things are not working out and is able to change course and avoid being a victim to circumstances that steal the opportunity to succeed.

Success requires a huge amount of self-discipline and perseverance. It requires constant reflection and awareness. Exceptional leaders are not afraid of failure and understand failure is something they can use to learn and grow from.

Success takes a lot of dedication and consistency. There are going to be many days of tears, challenges, mistakes, and hard days. Nothing in life is going to be easy or just happens for you or the people around you.

Exceptional leaders do not let bad moments steal opportunities or let them define them; they always bounce back and keep going until they physically can not anymore. Exceptional minds are some of the toughest warriors you will come across, and they leave the people and environments around them feeling challenged and focused. They speak in ways that empower and speak life into others.

Exceptional minds have a grit that makes them unstoppable and strong; they tend to be wonderful caring people with big hearts but also maintain a balance of character that also promotes growth, learning and offers composed environments where success can be born. Leaders with this mindset can also celebrate with their teams and can help them through the rough waters too.

Obstacles do not hold them back, and overall, they are always ready for challenge and change. Being an exceptional mind requires us to always be present and offers us optimal growth and innovative mindsets that create leaders wherever they go.

The exceptional mindset is a true act of compassion and can be achieved by anyone who strives to do their best and wants to be remembered for their extraordinary character and acts of bravery to succeed in a fast-paced world that demands our strength and solutions.

Bio Amanda M Renaud

Amanda is a 36-year-old leadership entrepreneur with three sons. She was born in Toronto, Ontario, but currently resides in the small town of Waubaushene, Ontario.

Amanda holds a degree in Child and Youth Treatment and is striving every day to become a well-recognized author across the globe in hopes of helping others, sharing and teaching others how to succeed. Amanda is a featured co-author in *For Women,* remarkable stories of survival, teaching others how to be true leaders and live a better way of life.

Amanda is a car accident survivor and suffers from a traumatic brain injury, but that has never stopped her from succeeding or helping others around her.

Amanda completed over seven years of rehabilitation therapy and never let her physical struggles or traumas stop her from accomplishing her goals. She has many years of leadership experience and has had a very unique walk of life. Amanda has had many struggles in her life but has worked very hard to become an inspirational leader everywhere she goes.

Amanda, despite her struggles, is the true definition of resilience and overcoming adversity and has demonstrated a vast knowledge of self-development. She hopes to one day change the world by showing others she is a highly motivated individual with a passion for reading and writing.

She is an entrepreneur, featured in *For Women,* a leadership collaboration, in 2019, and is eager to pursue her career as an inspiring author. Amanda showcases her knowledge and writing skills in both *For Women* and *Exceptional Minds.* She is a bright young lady with a sense of humour and plans to own a publishing company to help others get their message out to the world.

To contact Amanda:

Amanda M Renaud

(705) 427-2730